For you were there when the place was young — or younger— and so were you.
That's part of the dream-like quality. It's always young at Penn State. You feel a
bit of it in your blood, in the sniff of earth, of electrical dynamos and pungent
chem labs and dairy barns and in the brief and tantalizing scent of perfume
passing… Yes, there is a niceness about the place, this place favored above
many others, in a bowl of mountains, under a sky and an occasional freshening
wind, a place that everyone is glad to get to, glad to get away from, and can
never leave entirely or recapture.

Samuel Vaughan '51, Senior Vice President, Random House, in *The Penn Stater*, 1975

FOR THE
GLORY

REFLECTIONS OF PENN STATE

PHOTOGRAPHED BY LYNN JOHNSON

HARMONY HOUSE
PUBLISHERS LOUISVILLE

The Obelisk

Our thanks to the Penn State Alumni Association for all its help in the production of this book. In particular we wish to thank: William J. Rothwell, Ross B. Lehman, Marjory J. Sente, Sheryl Weinerman and Kathy Harford. In addition we wish to thank The Pennsylvania State University, particularly Bryce Jordan, William C. Richardson, George R. Lovette, Pete Kowalski, Mary Jo Haverbeck, Lee Stout, Cindy Ahmann, Sue Petro and John Vastyan.

Executive Editors: William Butler and William Strode
Director of Photography: William Strode
Hardcover International Standard Book Number 0-916509-21-4
Library of Congress Catalog Number 86-082743
Printed in USA by Gateway Press, Louisville, Kentucky
First Edition printed Fall, 1987 by Harmony House Publishers
P.O. Box 90, Prospect, Kentucky 40059 (502)228-2010 / 228-4446
Copyright © 1987 by Harmony House Publishers
Photographs copyright © 1987 Lynn Johnson

President Atherton's Grave

University House

INTRODUCTION

By Ross B. Lehman '42
Executive Director Emeritus
Penn State Alumni Association

I was a naive, unsophisticated, partly uncultured lad when I came to Penn State. As I entered the Nittany Valley, the first sight to greet me was the beautiful tower of Old Main. When I entered the classroom I encountered such unusual professors as Hum Fishburn, Nelson McGeary, Lou Bell, Bob Galbraith, and many others who exposed me to the awe of new worlds unfolding. They opened a door to challenging ideas, and another door beckoned, and another ... endless, and I felt that knowledge was forever moving and lasting in my life. If I had felt lonely and isolated in these hills it was not for long. I became part of the heart throb of Penn State, and it was a new, exciting world. I fell in love with this unique place.

The campus was, and is, something rather special. It houses the "Penn State spirit," which is a difficult thing to define because it is composed of so many things.

Perhaps it can be called a feeling, a feeling that runs through Penn Staters when they're away from this place and someone mentions "Penn State." The farther we are away, in time and distance, the stronger the feeling grows.

It is a good feeling, a wanting-to-share feeling. It is full of a vision of Mount Nittany, which displays a personality of its own in all its seasonal colors, from green to gold to brown to white. It is the sound of chimes from Old Main's clock, so surrounded by leaves that it's hard to see; it is getting to class not by looking at the clock but by listening to it.

It is the smell of the turf at New Beaver Field after a game, and the memories of Len Krouse, Leon Gajecki, Rosey Grier, Lenny Moore, Mike Reid, Franco Harris, Lydell Mitchell, Todd Blackledge and Curt Warner helping to swell our fame ... and the top of Mount Nittany as seen from the grandstands in autumn.

It is the quiet of Pattee Library, facing two rows of silent elms; sunlight falling gently through those elms on a misty morning; a casual chat under a white moon on the mall.

It is talk, too: a great deal of talk, here, there, all around ... in fraternity and sorority bull sessions or over a hasty coffee in the Corner Room or Ye Olde College Diner, talk un- recalled except for the feeling of remembrance and the heart-tugging wantings of youth.

Schwab Auditorium

It is the smell of a laboratory, the wondering about a tiny cell and its pattern — in its own tiny universe like that of a Milky Way galaxy — and the professor's scintillating comment that prompts a lone wrestling with a sudden intriguing but frightening thought about our awesome cosmos.

It is a dance in Rec Hall; a beer in the Rathskeller; a kiss in a secluded campus niche; the romance that bloomed into marriage; the smell of a theater; the laugh of a crowd; the blossoming of spring shrubs and the blend of maple, oak, birch and aspen colors in the fall; the ache of a night without sleep; and the sharing of a thousand other little things and incidents that honed our "Penn State spirit."

It is the flash of many faces and of the single one that touched our lives forever.

It is here that Penn State molds a person's life from the raw and unsophisticated into the conscious and cultured. We learned that a person must first be responsible to himself before he can be responsible to his university, his society, his world.

It is on this beautiful campus that we learn, as my wife Katey wrote," A man's soul and his life are his own, and even if he gives himself away in hundreds of careful and loving pieces, he's still his own man with his own life span, and no one but he has a claim on it, except his God."

And here, in this lovely, intriguing spot called Penn State, each of us staked our own special, precious and eventful life.

Penn State is a benediction to all of us who have graced these beautiful halls and malls.

PENN STATE HISTORICAL MILESTONES

1855 Farmers' High School of Pennsylvania is chartered.

1859 Farmers' High School opens to students; Dr. Evan Pugh becomes first president.

1861 First class graduates and is first to complete baccalaureate program at an American agricultural college; First graduate work is offered.

1862 Name changes to Agricultural College of Pennsylvania.

1863 Becomes Land Grant College; First master's degree is awarded.

1864 William Allen becomes 2nd president.

1866 Prof. John Fraser becomes 3rd president.

1868 Thomas H. Burrowes becomes 4th president.

1870 Alumni Association organizes.

1871 Dr. James Calder becomes 5th president; First women students are admitted.

1874 Name changes to The Pennsylvania State College.

1880 Dr. Joseph Shortlidge becomes 6th president.

1882 Dr. George Atherton becomes 7th president.

1887 Agriculture Experiment Station is established; Students publish first newspaper, *The Free Lance*; First state appropriations granted; Penn State beats Bucknell in first official intercollegiate football game.

1888 First fraternity (Phi Gamma Delta) receives charter.

1889 First *La Vie* is published.

1892 Correspondence course is offered in agriculture.

1899 The Blue Band begins.

1901 Trustees declare Pattee's *Alma Mater* official.

1907 Students adopt Nittany Lion as athletic symbol; Trustees officially accept it in 1942.

1908 Dr. Edwin Sparks becomes 8th president.

1910 *Froth* humor magazine is first published.

1912 Allentown Campus is founded as site of first classes held away from University Park.

1920 Alumni hold first Homecoming.

1921 Dr. John Thomas becomes 9th president.

1922 Graduate School is established.

1926 First Ph.D. is conferred on Marsh White.

1927 Dr. Ralph D. Hetzel becomes 10th president and serves in office 21 years.

1930 Old Main is rebuilt and opened; Mont Alto Forestry School is acquired for freshman instruction.

1931 Nittany Lion Inn opens.

1934 First permanent undergraduate centers open at Hazleton and Pottsville to begin Commonwealth Campus system.

1937 Phi Beta Kappa chapter is chartered.

1940 New library building is occupied; It is named for Fred Lewis Pattee in 1950; Student newspaper becomes *The Daily Collegian*.

1942 Nittany Lion Shrine is dedicated.

1949 Henry Varnum Poor completes Old Main frescos.

1950 Milton Eisenhower becomes 11th president.

1951 First Distinguished Alumnus Awards are presented.

1953 Name officially becomes The Pennsylvania State University.

1955 Breazeale Nuclear Research Reactor is dedicated; Hetzel Union Building is dedicated, and the University Park Post Office opens.

1956 Dr. Eric Walker becomes 12th president.

1958 Trustees create Woman of the Year award.

1959 Stone Valley Recreation Area is established (it opens in 1961); Undergraduate centers are designated Commonwealth Campuses.

1960 Beaver Stadium is completed; Evan Pugh Research Professorships are created.

1961 Study Abroad program is established.

1963 The Milton S. Hershey Medical Center founded.

1965 Penn State grants 100,000th degree; WPSX-TV begins broadcasting.

1967 Delaware County Campus opens, bringing total of Commonwealth Campuses to twenty.

1969 Women students are permitted to enroll in ROTC program.

1970 Dr. John W. Oswald becomes 13th president; Renaissance Fund is established.

1973 Behrend Campus is redesignated Behrend College; Alumni Fellows Program is established.

1974 Hershey Medical Center develops long-life rechargeable heart pacemaker, and implants it in first patient.

1976 Penn State confers 200,000th degree.

1978 Penn State researchers design heart assist pump.

1980 University Scholars program is initiated; Alumnus Paul Berg is co-winner of the 1980 Nobel Prize in Chemistry.

1982 Football team wins its first NCAA National Championship.

1983 Dr. Bryce Jordan becomes 14th president.

1985 Penn State artificial heart is implanted in first human.

1986 Campaign for Penn State is officially begun; Capitol Campus is designated Capital College.

1987 The football team wins its second National Championship.

Old Main

King of Prussia

While at Penn State, you were participants in a daring experiment in the history of human affairs: the free exchange of ideas. During your stay on this beautiful campus, you listened to, and expressed, many different theories and opinions that had to be rigorously examined and defended in pursuit of an elusive goal: the Truth.

Frank Stanton, Chairman, American National Red Cross, Commencement, 1977

Wilkes-Barre

From nuclear physics to highway engineering to medical research to agricultural development — Penn State has been the pilot light of progress and intellectual integrity in our third century as a Commonwealth. As a Pennsylvanian, I want to pay personal tribute to that record, to all who have contributed to it in the past, and to all who will do so in the future.

Governor Dick Thornburgh, Commencement , 1980

Ogontz

THE LIBRARY IS A SUM-
MONS TO SCHOLARSHIP

FINE ARTS
AND
LIBERAL ARTS

1938

Pattee Library

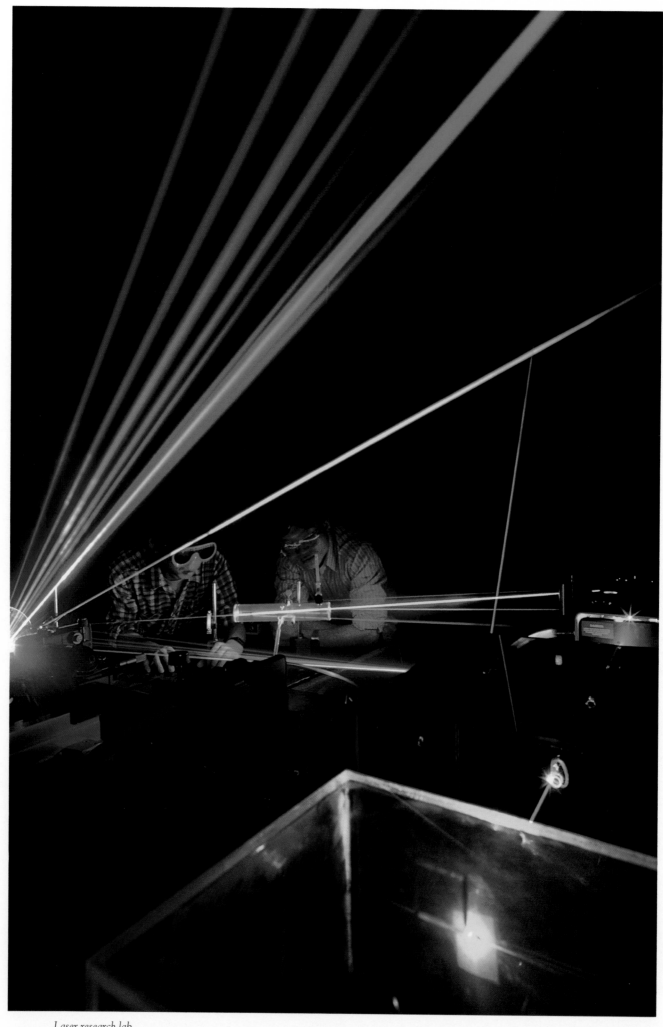

Laser research lab

Davey Lab

Berks

New Kensington

Berks

Worthington Scranton

Worthington Scranton

The Nittany Lion Inn

The Corner Room

We live by ourselves up in the mountains, and we have the best of opportunities both for study and for healthful recreation and social enjoyment.

John M. Thomas, Penn State president, in *La Vie*, 1926

The Creamery

West Halls

The Hub

Pollock Area

Penn State Heart

The Milton S. Hershey Medical Center

*(Penn State) will endeavor to secure that harmonious and symmetrical development
of all the faculties, which distinguishes the thoroughly educated from the half-educated.
Not simply the artisan, but the scholar; not simply the scholar, but the man.*

George W. Atherton, Inaugural address, 1883

Atmospheric research

I have been well acquainted over the years with a number of the faculty members of this institution and have good reason to know the significance and high quality of the extraordinary range of work, study and research carried on here.

Arthur S. Adams, President, American Council on Education, Commencement, 1954

Botanical research

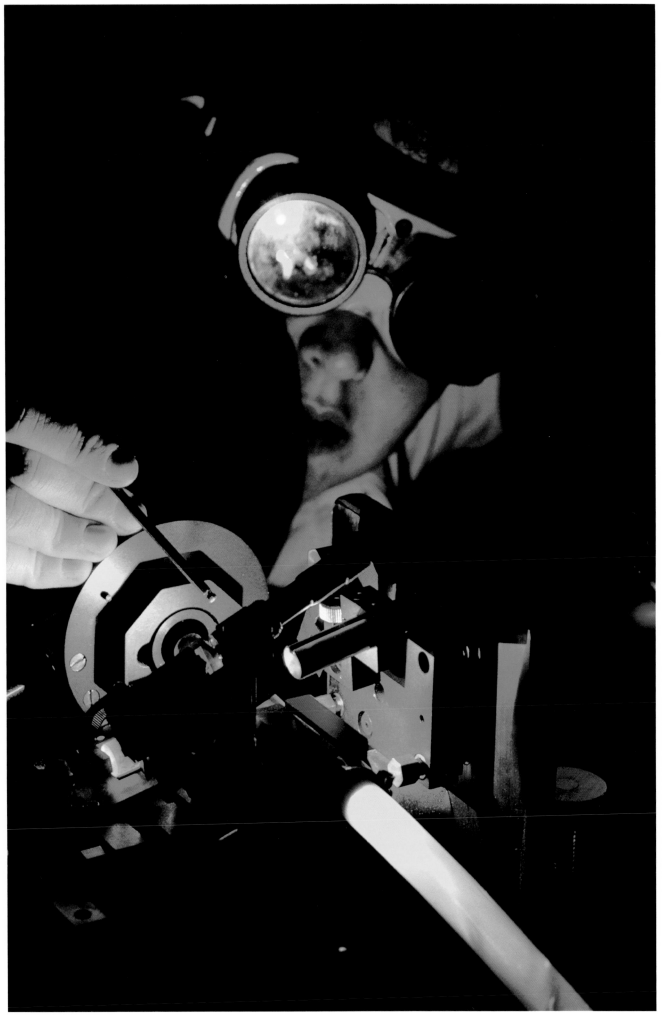

Schwab Auditorium

Carnegie Building

Hazleton

Altoona

Behrend College

WRESTLING

Stone Valley Recreation Area

How can one write in Happy Valley? If one doesn't let contentment with the scenery and the cultivation of one's garden or golf game get in the way, the opportunities are here.

Stanley Weintraub '56g, biographer and research professor of English, in *Town and Gown*, September, 1984

Land Grant Frescoes, Old Main

Who founds a College hall devote a Truth
Builds on eternal youth
Who builds where dawning manhood peers
With measuring eye adown the years,

Who raises by the path a shrine
To higher strivings dedicate and things divine
Builds for eternities,
And makes for evermore the future his.
This solid dome shall last
When thrones and kingdoms have been overcast.

Professor Fred Lewis Pattee, *The Message of the West*

Fayette

Shenango

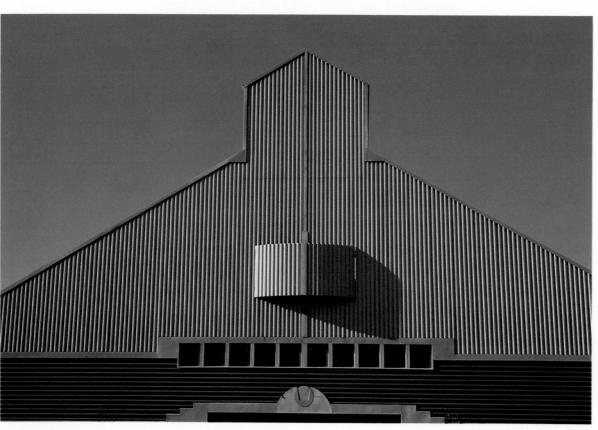

One of the characteristics which allows Penn State to stand apart from other universities
is the fact that here we have so many thousands and thousands of people living together
in a virtually isolated community. Even though we are such a large group, each of us is
a very distinct individual within that group, thinking our own thoughts and living our lives
in the way which is best for each of us.

Lesley Cohen '73, in *La Vie*, 1973

Delaware County

Mont Alto

Beaver

I've always hoped to be able to work in an atmosphere where the approach by the administration toward athletics was such that I can be more than a coach. That's what Penn State has allowed me to be. The overriding factor in my decision was my realization that I enjoy working with young people and having an influence over their lives.

Joe Paterno, Penn State head football coach

Homecoming

From the time of my entering Penn State in the fall of 1918 I hiked. Coming here, I had looked from a train window at the Bald Eagle Range, splotched then with the seared foliage of blighted chestnuts, seeing it as a wooded barrier beyond which lay a promised land. Once in the Nittany Valley itself, taking off into naturally wild and mountainous places would often seem a more delectable way of spending a color-drenched autumn afternoon than watching football from a packed bleacher.

Harold Dickson '22, professor emeritus of art history, in *Town and Gown*, 1979

*I know that friends and fans of the Nittany Lions take great
pride in athletic achievement, but it is especially gratifying
to know that this pride also extends to the fine record of aca-
demic prowess compiled by Penn State players over the years.
Your football alumni have made great contributions in the
arts, literature, science, entertainment, business, politics,
and professional sports.*

*This commitment to excellence both on and off the field is
in keeping with the historic mission of your school, and it
is a tribute to your concern for the total well-being of the
young people who participate in athletics at Penn State.
The values learned on the football field — discipline,
preparation, teamwork, self-sacrifice and good sports-
manship — make not only for victories and champion-
ships in autumn, but for triumphs in all of life's seasons.*

President Ronald Reagan, July 1986

Capital College

York

Schuylkill

Allentown

McKeesport

Wilkes-Barre

DuBois

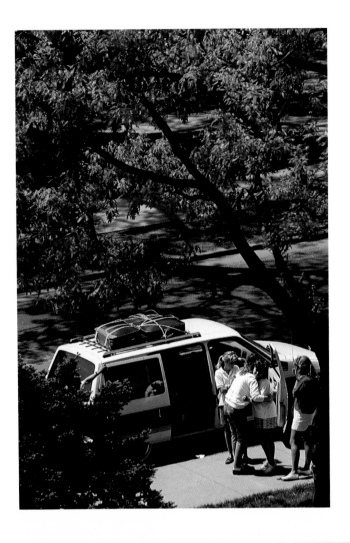

Recent accomplishments, honors, and initiatives
throughout the institution instill the pride of a job well
done. Yet in every Penn State achievement there is a
new challenge. Such is the nature of learning, to
which the University is dedicated above all else. Each
frontier of knowledge gives way to another. There is
always a mind stretching farther than ever before.

Bryce Jordan, President's Report 1983-1987

Who ever said you can't go home again? It was October 4, Homecoming, and there I was after eighteen years — eating breakfast in the Corner Room, listening to "Old Main" chime the quarter hours, and walking down the tree-lined malls. Tears streamed down my face. They were tears of happiness, of joyful memories. Everything was the same — maybe bigger, but the same. Spaghetti at the Tavern, beer parties at the fraternity houses, and my messy sorority suite. Beaver Stadium, the Blue Band, the Alma Mater...Yes, Dear Old State, it's true — "Thou didst mold us into men."

Doris Frank Jedel '57, in *The Penn Stater*, 1976